NETWORK LIKE A PRO

Building Valuable Contacts and Connections

By
Kim Brushaber

About the Author

Kim Brushaber was social from a very young age. When her parents used to throw parties, Kim preferred to go out and talk with the adults rather than play with the other children. Her parents guests would remark how well spoken she was. She truly enjoyed the art of conversation.

In high school, Kim surrounded herself with multiple circles of friends. She enjoyed the nerds, the jocks, the popular crowd, the band geeks, the drama club and the misfits. While these groups didn't normally interact with each other outside of class, Kim enjoyed splitting her time amongst them all.

In college, Kim was part of a student organization that was supposed to cater only to her major. She realized that the programming could be beneficial to students across campus. During her the time when she was membership officer she took this student organization from 150 paid members to over 500 paid members (a feat that has never been done again since).

Kim spent the early part of her career as a "techie" working in a variety of different aspects of the software development lifecycle. While she enjoyed the work very much she never quite figured out how to bring the socialization aspect into her work environment. She continued to be the hub for all information surrounding a group of about fifty of her friends from college.

In 2008, Kim left the tech world to enter the world of recruiting. Here she excelled in networking. Within a six month period she went from 300 trusted contacts on LinkedIn to over 650 trusted contacts. These were all people that she met and interacted with on a regular basis. She frequently found herself quadruple booked for networking events in the evenings and would normally make it to all of them.

In 2009, Kim decided to launch her own company, Bridge ATX. Amongst other things she realized that there was a real need for entrepreneurs and job seekers to be able to network more effectively. She started hosting "Connection Conversations". The networking aspect of this work was translated into an hour long workshop called "Network Like A Pro" which was attended by several hundred people through a variety of events hosted over two years. She also launched a presentation that she was able to give when speaking at events.

Kim's network of what she considers personal friends now includes 850 Facebook friends and over 1600 LinkedIn contacts. She is truly one of the queens of Austin networking.

Acknowledgements

Although it is impossible to acknowledge every person I have encountered as a job seeker or a hiring manager, I would like to take a moment to thank a few specific people without whom this journey would not have been possible.

Special thanks to my copy editors – Greg Effrein, Larry Wallace, Jan Hames and Bill Herring

Another special thanks to Mark Thames, without whom I would not have been sparked to post this workbook online for all to use

To all the people who have ever attended one of my "Network Like a Pro" conversations

I would also like to acknowledge my family, without whom I would not have had the ambition to write this book.

TABLE OF CONTENTS

Network Like A Pro

Currently, networking is a prevalent buzz word. There are thousands and thousands of articles available that tell you that you should be networking and building valuable contacts. While you know you should be networking, few people actually know how to get started. It is true that there are natural networkers who walk into a room and instantly make friends or perhaps already know everyone in the room. There are also magical people who are able to remember the most intricate details about their last conversation like your most recent trip or your children's most recent birthday. These unicorns of the happy hour world are rare to find but there tends to be at least one in every crowd. So, what do you do if you are not one of these natural networkers? I'm here to help.

Have you ever found yourself at an event where you walk into a room and there are 200 people in it and you know no one there? You scan the room looking for the sight of a familiar face. Seeing none, your palms begin to sweat. You feel uncomfortable and you nervously back away to the nearest wall to survey the room. You wish you had brought someone to talk to, but you didn't think ahead. If there's a bar at the event, you head to it, hoping to muster some liquid courage. You spot one slightly familiar face but they are in a group of people who are already talking to each other and you don't want to interrupt. It appears as though everyone is grouped together in a prearranged clique that you have been left out of. Someone finally takes pity on you because they see that you are alone and they begin a conversation that you couldn't care less about, but at least you are not alone. You cling to this uninteresting person for 20 minutes until you can't stand it anymore. You rush to escape this dreadful event. Once you are out of the event venue, you feel terrible –like you completely wasted your time. And in fact, you did waste your time because you didn't meet a single other soul other than the one who bored you to tears. You silently swear that you will never go back to another networking event again.

If this story makes you break out into a cold sweat just thinking about it. You are not alone. Even as much as I network and as much as I practice, I will occasionally find myself in this odd situation. Fortunately, I know how to salvage the event. However for many people, they live this story every time they go out networking. I promise whether you are an expert networker or a novice, the pages in this workbook will help you to overcome your networking challenges, so that you can "Network Like a Pro".

Why Should You Network

Dictionary.com defines networking (how I use the term) as – "a supportive system of sharing information and services among individuals and groups sharing a common interest."

This is the way that networking should work. Unfortunately, for most people they do not feel as though they have a support system of people to network with. I will help you to change that.

There are a variety of reasons why you should network. Human beings network all the time (even the most introverted). People are social by nature. We need human contact or we will die. Most people do not have a problem interacting one on one with someone, especially if they know them already. There are some people who are truly fascinated and captivated by the experience of meeting new people. Many people are, terrified meeting a crew of strangers. So, why would you want to actively network if it is such a scary experience?

You have picked up this workbook with a purpose. What are your reasons for wanting to network?

_____

_____

_____

_____

_____

_____

_____

_____

Here are my top three reasons that I believe people want to network – Information, Interaction and Influence. Can you tell I love alliteration?

Information

The first most valuable thing you can gather from networking is Information. The Internet and Google have made gathering information less of a necessity. However, there is no search engine out there that can replace the collective knowledge of a group of people. As adults, we have had many years of experience learning a variety of different things. No two people have walked in the same shoes for every moment of every day, processing information in the same way. Even if two people have acquired the same information, different people have different perspectives on how to interpret that information. While not every conversation is earth shattering, each conversation can potentially be the key to unlock the door about something that you have been wondering about.

While there are many different ways to network, networking events are the most common way to get out and meet new people.

- For people who are in a sales or marketing capacity networking events can provide a wealth of information towards market research or lead generation.
- For people who are looking for a new job, networking events can provide insight into companies and contacts that they need to meet. It is also possible to meet a hiring manager at a networking event.
- For all individuals, networking events can provide new insight and information about topics that interest them.

What kind of information would you like to get out of networking?

Influence

Networking gives you an opportunity to influence others, and to be influenced by them. Meeting more people creates visibility for whatever you are trying to accomplish. Networking lets people promote in a socially acceptable way. People might want to promote themselves to find a new job, promote a vision, a perspective, or a cause.

There are ways to influence in both a positive or negative way. I will discuss more about "Nasty Networking" later in this workbook for a perspective on the negative way to influence people.

How much are you able to positively influence other people while networking?

___

Interaction

Networking is no more than interacting with other people. You do it at school, you do it at work, and you do it at home. If you strike up a conversation with someone in the aisle behind you at the grocery store, you are networking.

Networking can lead to an amazing ability to collaborate with individuals who you might not meet otherwise. While some people argue that competition is the main thing driving individuals, I would argue that it is the need to cooperate and collaborate.

And sometimes, networking is purely about the desire to get out and meet new people, to be stimulated by new faces, new thoughts, and new perspectives.

How do you want to interact with the people you meet while networking?

___

Types of Networking

The most frequent form of networking is done via Networking Events. These are events that are set up where you already may know people there or where you can meet new r people. This workbook goes into great detail about how to interact with people at networking events.

However, the reality is that every time you interact with someone there is a potential to network with them. You could network with someone who is in line behind you at the grocery store or beside you on an airplane. You could network with another parent at your children's soccer game or dance recital. You could network with someone via Social Media. You could network with someone over coffee or lunch. You could network with someone via an old fashioned letter.

The reality is that when you spend time meeting someone and then decide to support them (or they decide to support you) in their interests then you are networking.

See if you can think of ten times over the last month where you were networking and you may not have even realized you were doing it.

Networking Is Not

While networking can have several definitions, there are some things that networking is not. Networking is not an instant return, your personal sales pitch, or a popularity contest. Time and again, I find that people go to networking events seeking these elements and find themselves shunned or disgruntled when their actions take a negative turn.

An Instant Return

On rare occasions, you will meet someone and after 20 minutes you will feel like you have known them forever. However, in most cases relationships and trust are built over a period of time. Many people hear that networking can find them a job or a business lead and they set out for the night expecting great rewards.

I throw a monthly networking event where there is no defined purpose other than to meet other nice people. While it is true that occasionally someone comes to my networking event and finds another individual who was looking for their talents, this rarely occurs. At one point my networking events were getting the reputation that people were finding jobs. I started to get negative feedback from the job seeking community; some attendees personally attacked me because they didn't find their next job at the event. After getting over my initial shock of upsetting someone (I'm a natural people pleaser), I realized that I could have a real problem on my hands if people broadly thought that my networking events were magically finding people jobs. I talked to people I knew within the job seeking community and they all assured me that my message was not being miscommunicated. Instead, the individuals themselves were desperate, and pinning all their hopes on finding a job at a single networking event.

More often than not, people will come to my networking event one month and they will meet some new people. The next month they return because they had a good experience the first month. At the next month's event they will make new connections, but they will also reinforce the connections they have already made. New information and insights will be shared and rapport will start to grow. Then as people go and spread out from my networking event, their new connections will meet new people and they will think of the individuals from my events and facilitate introductions on their behalf. Many of the job seekers that attend my events find jobs in this fashion. They met someone at my event who introduces them to someone who introduces them to someone else who introduces them to the person who hires them.

Whether you are looking for a job or you are just looking to meet new people, understand that it takes time to build solid connections. Each and every networking event works to strengthen those connections and bonds with the people you meet.

Your Personal Sales Pitch

I will get further into this conversation when I approach the subject of "Nasty Networkers." Briefly, a networking event is not an opportunity to make a sales pitch. I see it happen over and over again with people who are new to networking. People hear that you can get new sales if they go to networking events. It is true that at some networking events you are given 30 seconds to a minute to introduce yourself and give out your pitch. It is also true that some people choose to host a networking event in order to sell you something. However, without people knowing in advance that they are going to be pitched to, they are not going to be comfortable if you ramble on about whatever it is that you are trying to sell.

Think of the terrible reputation that so many timeshare companies have achieved. You lure someone to a beautiful exotic location. You spend a full day of their vacation on a hard sell convincing them to invest in a condo that they can come and visit anytime they want. While we all know what timeshare companies are doing (and most of us won't accept their free vacations for anything), think of the first few people who were enticed to do so with no knowledge of what they were getting into. It leaves a bad taste in your mouth and makes you feel like a mark.

So, if someone is going to a networking event with the idea that they are going to meet new and interesting people, imagine how they will feel when you start to break into a conversation about how they really need to invest in some life insurance. Ick!

Save your reputation and don't pitch to someone at a networking event. It's perfectly reasonable for you to assess someone's interest in a topic and set up a time outside of the event to meet. But do not walk away from the one and only conversation that you might have with an individual leaving a bad impression.

A Popularity Contest

While this may sound funny coming from someone who has developed a large quantity of connections over time, networking events are not a popularity contest. Your end goal should never be to meet as many people as you possibly can. Collecting the most business cards does not make you the best networker. I've seen so many people come back from networking events with giant stacks of business cards and they have no memory of the people they met or anything significant about them. The true value of networking is completely lost.

Instead, it is important go to a networking event with the intention to make as many valuable connections as you can make during the time you have. This means that you need to invest time and energy into your conversations.

Common Concerns

As I talk to people about their worries surrounding networking, there are a few main themes.

1) **Swimming in A Giant Sea of People**
2) **Not Knowing Anyone / Talking to Strangers**
3) **Getting Value for your Time**
4) **Not Knowing what to Say**
5) **Speaking with a Group of People**
6) **Fear of Rejection**
7) **Getting Rid of Someone**
8) **Being Afraid to Ask For Help**
9) **Networking without a Voice**

Okay, so most people don't encounter #9, but I have, so I decided to share it. I'll give you ways to combat all of these scenarios as we continue our conversation.

Not to worry, though. This workbook will address these concerns and more and have you feeling like a natural networker before you know it.

Are there any other concerns that you have with networking? List them below.

_____

_____

_____

_____

_____

_____

_____

_____

Networking Etiquette (No Nasty Networkers)

I had a friend who was particularly good at networking. He put out a survey to several of his friends to find out what they think are the qualities of a "Nasty Networker." A Nasty Networker is someone you encounter at a networking event that you just can't wait to be free of. While I can't remember all of the things that came up in his survey, here are some of the Nasty Networker behaviors that I encounter and would love see you avoid.

Behavior	Remedy
Tossing your Business Cards Around to Everyone	We all want to make sure that people have our contact information so that they can get back to us. However, some people don't wait until appropriate rapport has been built before they hand out their business card and go onto the next conversation. Wait to hand out your business card to people until either they ask for it OR the conversation has been concluded.
Talking Too Much	We've all met people who love to hear themselves talk. Everyone is waiting for them to take a breath so they can bolt from the conversation. In order to keep you from being one of those people, take frequent one second pauses in order to allow room for comment. If you feel that you have been talking for an extensive amount of time, stop and give the other person a chance to interject. Remember rapport is best built when people feel they've shared something of themselves with you and in turn, learned something of who you are.
Interrupting Conversations	When you are having a great conversation with someone, it's disturbing to have someone come up and start talking about a completely different topic... In order to keep yourself from being one of those people, wait for a natural pause in conversation to introduce yourself or interject.
Drinking Too Much	Many people use alcohol in order to make networking events more tolerable for them. Sometimes at events, people will even buy drinks for you in order to keep the conversation going. There comes a point where drinking becomes more of a hindrance than a benefit. Before you go to the event, consider your personal alcohol tolerance and decide how much you can drink and still carry on a conversation that you will remember. Then be sure to keep count of your drinks and drink one less than you think you'll be able to.

It's All About Me	Many people go to networking events only thinking about the things that they are looking to get out of the networking event. They overlook the fact that networking is a give and take activity. I help you and you help me. Make sure that while you are communicating what you are looking for, you also take time to learn about the things that the other person is looking for.
Mud Slinging	People don't go to networking events to hear people say bad things about other people or companies. Use Thumper's Rule from Bambi "If you can't say something nice, don't say anything at all."
Bad Attitude	Not everyone is perky "Mary Sunshine." However, if you frequently go to networking events in a bad mood, you will become the "Debbie Downer" of the group. Try to be upbeat and positive as much as you can. If you can't be upbeat and positive, just be willing to listen to what the other person is talking about.
Being Disrespectful, Rude or Impolite	While every culture has different perceptions on what are disrespectful, rude or impolite, people generally know what acceptable behavior for their environment is. If you are networking within a new culture, watch other people's behaviors and actions until you get an understanding for what the proper customs and behavior are.

If all else fails, live by the Golden Rule – Treat Others as You Would Like To Be Treated – at a networking event.

What other qualities have you seen "Nasty Networkers" portray?

_____

_____

_____

_____

_____

_____

Setting Goals

Networking is much easier if you set some goals before you go out to a networking event. Talking with many of my friends who are out networking all the time has helped me consolidate all networking goals into one of five different categories. The novice networkers I know who are terrified of networking have all agreed that these are reasonable goals that they can achieve at a networking event.

These goals are:

- Practice Networking
- Build Rapport
- Gather Information
- Target Companies or Industries
- Target Individuals

I encourage you to pick one goal and stick with it until you can comfortable meet that goal at multiple networking events. Combining too many goals can be overwhelming and cause you not to meet any of them. Having a goal in advance can make the difference between leaving a networking event feeling lost or feeling successful.

I once went to a networking event where I had three goals in mind. First, I wanted to meet ten new contacts. Second, I wanted to build rapport amongst the people I already knew. Third, because I was single I wanted to meet a nice man who I could possibly date in the future This example was a two hour event where I thought that surely I could accomplish all of my tasks. I started the night spotting a very cute boy with a British Accent who I wanted to get a date with. We were having a great conversation when a girlfriend of mine came over and introduced herself. As time went on I had several other friends come up to us.

I realized about an hour into the event that I hadn't been paying much attention to the guy because my friends kept coming up and interrupting us. I also realized that I hadn't talked to a single person that I didn't already know. So I excused myself from the conversation and went to attempt to talk to ten new people in the course of an hour. This meant that I had six minutes to talk to each new person and try to establish enough of a rapport with them that I could walk away knowing something significant about them. People I knew continued to come up and talk to me when I was meeting new people. Unfortunately, I spent the whole event watching my girlfriend talk to the cute boy with the British Accent and I didn't pay much attention to any of the other people around me.

At the end of the night, I felt like it was a total flop. Although I was able to talk to some of the people that I already knew, I lost the boy to my girlfriend and I didn't remember a single thing that anyone new to me said that night. Instead of three goals, I should have committed myself to just one of them that night in order to meet my objective. People wonder how I can meet so many people and still be single. That night showed me why.

Let's look further into each of these networking goals and why one goal can occupy a whole networking event.

Practice Networking

If you aren't particularly skilled at networking, you'll want to set up a few events where you can meet people. Your main goal may be to meet people and help break yourself out of your shell. You can feel comfortable doing this because you know that your main task at this event is to go up and meet people without any hidden objectives. It's perfectly okay to tell people that you are new to networking and ask for help in figuring out the ropes. This is a great time to try out a new way of introducing yourself.

If you are at a networking mixer (meaning everyone is just walking around talking to each other for two hours), a reasonable goal is to practice by having conversations with at least ten people.

Choose a networking event to go to where you know that there will be at least ten people who don't know you already where you can go and "Practice Networking". Come back to the workbook and fill out the section below.

What were your thoughts and impressions before you went to the networking event?

What were your thoughts and impressions upon returning from the networking event?

What new things did you learn about the people you met?

What new things did you learn about yourself after the event?

What can you do better next time in order to be even more effective networking?

Building Rapport

While building rapport can be done with someone who you've just met, this is a better goal for repeating an event that you have been to before. For this goal, your primary mission is to get to know someone better. You learn a little bit more about them as they learn a little bit more about you.

I was once at a networking event when I heard a good friend of mine introduce himself to someone new. In this new introduction he brought up the fact that he grew up in Dallas, Texas. I also grew up in Dallas, Texas. I asked him why I didn't know that already and he simply said that it had never come up. We formed a new bond because a few moments later we discovered that we had graduated from the same high school five years apart from each other. You never know when you might learn something new and different about one another.

For a two hour networking mixer, I suggest that you find at least ten people who you already know and get to know them better.

Try and choose a networking event where you already know 10 people and "Build Rapport. Come back to the workbook and fill out the section below.

What were your thoughts and impressions before you went to the networking event?

What were your thoughts and impressions upon returning from the networking event?

What did you learn about the ten people that you already know?

What new information do these ten individuals learned about you?

What can you do better next time in order to be even more effective networking?

Gathering Information

Information gathering is another great networking goal. You should pick this goal when there is something you want to find out more about, such as a topic or industry. To be successful in information gathering, provide a focus in what you are looking for which may help them to help you. Don't give them the long list of all of the different ways that they can help you. Instead, give them something easy to think about and see if they can help.

I was working in recruiting and I wanted to learn more about the gaming industry in Austin. I found it to be an interesting industry and I wanted to find out if I might be able to help them find better candidates for their roles. So, I went out to every networking event for a week and I asked everyone I came into contact with if they knew something about this underground gaming industry in Austin. I quickly discovered that at the time Austin had fifty gaming studios that I knew nothing about. I learned that their main complaint when it came to staffing was that none of the recruiters that were working with them were local so they didn't understand the local talent scene.

If information gathering is your goal for a networking event, I suggest at a two hour mixer that you find at least five people who can give you helpful information on the topic that you are interested in. This means that you will likely have to talk to two to three times more people than that because many people will have no new information to provide you (and that's okay).

What are five things that you might like to gather information about at a networking event?

Choose a networking event to go to where you know that there will be at least ten people who don't know you already where you can "Gather Information". Come back to the workbook and fill out the section below.

What were your thoughts and impressions before you went to the networking event?

What were your thoughts and impressions upon returning from the networking event?

What new information did you gather?

Describe your ease or difficulty in gathering this information.

For your next event, what information will you gather based on what you know now?

What can you do better next time in order to be even more effective networking?

Targeting Companies or Industries

If you have identified a targeted company that you are interested in, your goal is to work the room and find anyone who knows someone at that company. Every connection is a possible doorway into that company. You may find someone who actually works for the company. However, you are really just looking for an introduction to someone with a connection to the company.

One day I was talking to a job seeker that I had been working with. She was overwhelmed by trying to target companies or individuals at a networking event. She was afraid of all the rejection she was going to receive when people would not have the information that she was after. So, I told her this scenario. Imagine that you are at a networking event and you are given the name of a famous couple and you are supposed to go around that networking event to find your other half. All of the names are given out at random so even knowing the person's sex does not mean you will find the person you are looking for. You are given the name "Wilma Flintstone," so you know that you are on a search to find "Fred Flintstone." You walk up to the first person and say, "Are you Fred Flintstone?" and they say, "No, I'm Marilyn Monroe." You walk up to the second person and say, "Are you Fred Flintstone?" and they say, "No, I'm that Chick Bella from Twilight." As you proceed around the room you finally find someone who says, "No, I'm not Fred, but I met Fred a few minutes ago. He's wearing a blue shirt." As you scan the sea of blue shirts, you ask another person and he says, "No, I'm not Fred, but I know who Fred is. Let me introduce you to him. Come with me."

I asked the struggling job seeker if the above scenario is something that would frighten her. She said that initially she probably would still be scared. However, after talking to the first few people, she would start to get the hang of it. I asked her if the fact that the people she talked to were not Fred Flintstone meant that she felt personally rejected by them. She told me "of course not." So then I asked why she felt like asking people for other forms of information seemed so intimidating. She thought about it for a while and realized that it is exactly the same thing. Sometimes the people you meet will be able to give you information about a target company and sometimes they won't. At the end of the day, if you have found Fred Flintstone, then you have met your goal. It didn't seem so scary anymore.

For this goal, see if you can identify at least five people at a networking event that can give you information about a company that you are targeting. Don't think you have to get introduced to them at the event. Simply ask that they give you an introduction at a later point in time that is convenient for both of you.

If you have several companies or industries that you are targeting, limit the list to 3 – 5 items before asking for help. When the list is too long, people won't be able to keep it in memory.

What are ten companies or industries that you would like to have more information on? Make a notation by the top 3 – 5 on your list.

Try and choose a networking event to go to where there will be at least ten people where you can go and ask questions about your target company or industry. Come back to the workbook and fill out the section below.

What were your thoughts and impressions before you went to the networking event?

What were your thoughts and impressions upon returning from the networking event?

What information did you discover about the company or industry that you were targeting?

For the next event, how can you make it easier to gather the information that you were looking for?

What can you do better next time in order to be even more effective networking?

Targeting Individuals

Sometimes there is a specific individual that you are looking to talk to. They may be a speaker or they on the board for the organization sponsoring a networking event. In this case, your main mission is to find some time to talk to that individual. You probably won't get a lot of time to talk to them, but you can at least introduce yourself, make yourself memorable (in a good way) and agree to follow up later.

I have this happen to me a lot because I host my own networking events. Frequently I will have someone contact me that I have not met and they would like some time to meet with me and talk to me. I always suggest that they come to one of my events. This way I can talk to them for a few minutes to determine if there is any reason for us to meet outside of the initial conversation. I save myself a lot of time because many of these people have just been told they need to meet me without a real reason to do so. However, sometimes these people are definitely people I need to meet. I can normally only talk to them for a few minutes but it's enough to establish the need to meet and talk later. They also get the benefit of meeting with all the other people at the event.

If you are looking to meet with a targeted individual, then your goal for the event is simply to get 45 seconds to talk to that person to see if there is any reason to have a further conversation.

If you could identify five people that you realistically think you could meet who would they be, why and where might you find them? Do not put Albert Einstein on this list, he's dead. Unless you have some great entertainment connections, don't put Lady Gaga on here either. Think about people who run companies that you're interested in. Think about people who represent organizations that you want to volunteer at. Think about people who run events that have topics that you're interested in. If you don't know the individual's name, that's okay too. If you don't have a top five list, you can always come back to it later when you've had more practice networking.

Who   Why   Where

Try and choose a networking event where you can go and "Target an Individual". Please don't interpret this to mean that you should become a hired assassin. Instead, find someone who you want to spend a short amount of time with and discuss an opportunity to meet up at a future date and time. Come back to the workbook and fill out the section below.

What were your thoughts and impressions before you went to the networking event?

What were your thoughts and impressions upon returning from the networking event?

Briefly describe your interaction with the individual.

If you agreed to meet in the future, what are the topics you'd like to see covered?

What can you do better next time in order to be even more effective networking?

Networking Preparation

Before you go to an event there are things that you should consider (other than your goals:

- Business Cards
- Elevator Pitch
- An Approachable Attitude
- Know your Availability

Business Cards

If you meet someone at a networking event, you should always have a way for them to be able to contact you. At most professional networking events, it is perfectly acceptable to trade business cards. I can't tell you how many times I've had a great conversation with someone only to want to continue the conversation and they don't have a way for me to get in contact with them. Sometimes I'll ask for their email and send them an email from my smart phone so we can follow up from there. Sometimes I'll ask them to write their information on the back of one of my business cards. However, I always like to get a physical business card from someone because it allows me to make notations on the back of the card as to when I met them and what we might have in common that would create a future conversation. I also note anything we might have talked about to jog my memory at a future date. It also helps to remind me to follow up with someone.

Because I always carry a stack of business cards with me, I know that people will be able to get in touch with me. This helps me to identify which people are really interested in having a further conversation with me.

Be careful not to accidentally give someone else's card away when you hand someone your business card. I like to keep one pocket for my cards and another pocket for the cards that I receive. This means if you don't have a purse, you should wear something with useable pockets to your networking events.

If you don't work for a company, you can still have your own cards printed. Vista Print will print cards for free as long as they can advertise on the back of your card. You can also go to an office supply store and get sheets of card stock that you can use to print out these cards. Free templates are available online that you can use to create a card that is uniquely yours.

Elevator Pitch

Further in the workbook, I will go over some different ways to introduce yourself at a networking event. In addition, I encourage that everyone prepare something that they will say in response to meeting someone that can occupy about 30 seconds of a conversation. This doesn't have to be your whole life story. It is simply something to start a conversation.

At networking events, you should always introduce yourself to someone new. It is important to have an objective in mind for that event, so be prepared to state what that is. For job seekers and entrepreneurs, this is an essential part of networking. For others, this is your opportunity to guide the conversation to something that interests you.

While I will admit that someone who is prepared and polished can easily guide the course of a conversation with a good elevator pitch, anyone should be able to come up with 30 seconds of something to say about themselves.

Consider:

- What do you do for a living?
- Where did you grow up?
- What are your favorite hobbies?
- Why are you out networking?
- What topics occupy your thoughts?

The key is not to tell people everything about you. Instead, give them something to continue the conversation with.

For example, I might say:

Hello, I'm Kim Brushaber. I spent twelve years working as a java programmer. I decided that my job was not social enough for me. I also wanted to do something that would directly help people on an everyday basis. I discovered I was really good at networking. I even decided to write a book about it. What do you do?

What items would you include in your elevator pitch?

What starting points might you be able to use to start a conversation with someone? Remember to keep it simple, short and sweet.

An Approachable Attitude

As I said before, no one likes to network with a "Debbie Downer." Before you go out to a networking event, make sure that your attitude is in check. Of course, we all have times where things are upsetting us and getting us down. Sometimes networking events can help us work through the problems that perplex us. However, even if you have a problem that you are trying to solve, I encourage you to keep an upbeat swing in all your networking conversations. Know that by going to this event you will be helping yourself.

I have a friend who was a little bit introverted. When I first met this friend, he was standing by himself against the wall, looking at his feet. He was terrified that someone might come up to him and he would have nothing to say. Never wanting to see anyone so miserable, I went up to him and started a conversation. I asked him what his name was. I asked him what he did for a living. I asked him what he enjoyed doing for fun. He was nervous; it was all he could do to answer me with one word responses. I looked at him and said, "Tell me about you and why you are here." He said that he had just moved to Austin from Seattle and that he needed to make some new friends. That made me remember that I had just met another person at the event who also came from Seattle. I told him to wait where he was and that I would be right back with her. I brought my other new friend back and the two of them started talking. They started to get animated reminiscing about things in Seattle. They even discovered that they had a few friends in common. Before long, both of them were smiling and laughing and other people were joining in on their conversation. I would have never known to bring the two of them together had he not said the one thing that sparked the connection. He ended up making several friends that night who have now helped him to make Austin feel like home.

Things turned out well for this friend of mine. It happened because I took the initial step over to speak to him. No one else in the room thought to do it. He looked so miserable no one wanted to talk to him. He could have easily have started that conversation with the girl from Seattle on his own had he been willing to smile a little bit and walk around and talk to people. He didn't need me – neither does anyone else. As soon as he started to smile, he warmed up the entire room. At networking events, it's all about your attitude.

On the flipside, I have several friends who are friendly and always laughing. Every time you look around the room they have people surrounding them wanting to be part of their stories. A simple smile and a reputation for being friendly are all you need in order to get people to come and talk to you at an event.

Know Your Availability

When you're at a networking event, you should always know a few times over the next week or so when you would be available to further a conversation. You might have time over lunch, coffee, or happy hour. You never know when you might meet someone at an event that you want to continue the conversation later. If you can supply them with a preferred meeting time at that moment, then you can save yourself time in follow up. The other person also needs to know their own schedule, but if you have several times to throw out, they normally can come up with one or two times that will work for them as well.

Networking Without a Voice

Removing the pressure to say something at a networking event would seem like a great benefit for most people. I am capable of jabbering like a monkey in a tree. Rarely do I find a topic that I can't contribute to. I also enjoy probing questions to help me to understand more about the individuals that I am networking with. The day I woke up without a voice before a networking event was cruel and unusual punishment. I'll share with you how I was able to take it in stride.

One morning I awoke without a voice. While this may not have been a big deal on most mornings, this particular morning I was going to be attending a networking event that I had never been to before. The event was hosting over a hundred female entrepreneurs. This was my target audience and I only knew a handful of the women attending the event. I knew I needed to find a good way to introduce myself without using my voice.

I sat down before the event and printed out two statements and pasted them to 4x6 index cards.

The first one read:

Please excuse me. I seem to have misplaced my voice today. You don't know me yet, but when you do you will know that this is one of the worst moments of my life. I can be quite the chatterbox. I was really looking forward to sharing a conversation with you. I hope that you will allow me to introduce myself. My name is Kim Brushaber. I am the CEO of Bridge ATX. I connect individuals to Austin businesses and Austin businesses to the Austin community. I started my own business in 2009. I assist people in helping them to understand their passion in life. Once their passion is determined, I help them to take the next steps to turn their passion into a career. Being an entrepreneur yourself I'm sure that you can understand passion. I also assist companies in helping them to improve their hiring processes in order to hire the best possible candidates. If you know anyone who is looking to make a career change or wants to make better hiring decisions, I would appreciate an introduction. Please let me know if you would like my business card.

The second one read:

Now that I have told you about myself I would like to get to know you better. Since I don't have a voice to carry a conversation I hope that you won't mind if I ask you a few questions. Please feel free to answer as many or as few as you would like.

1) Please tell me what you do.
2) What made you decide to do that?
3) If you could go back in time what would you warn yourself about?
4) What defines your target audience?
5) How can I help you?
6) Can I have your business card?

I could have to silently walked around the event picking up bits of information. I could have stayed close to my friends and allow them to speak on my behalf. Instead I wanted to be able to go and walk around the room and meet new people. I quickly summarized exactly what I wanted them to know about me. I was able to really listen. When I did run into my friends in a group of people they were able to introduce me and I was able to really listen to how they chose to describe me. There was the added benefit of people being able to read my notes in an otherwise very noisy room. It turned out to be a huge success. In fact, I wonder why I don't pretend to be mute more often.

Talking to Strangers

Lots of people are scared to talk to strangers. This is probably because when we were little, our parents told us not to talk to strangers and we didn't get much practice in doing so. While those warnings were used to keep us out of danger when we were little, we don't need them anymore as an adult. The reality is that strangers are people just like us and most of them are nothing to be scared of.

You Do it Every Day

Unless you have grown up in a very small town where everyone knows each other, you talk to strangers every single day. When you order a burger at a drive through, you are probably talking to a stranger. When you buy milk at the grocery store, you are probably talking to a stranger. There are all kinds of moments during the day where you find yourself talking to strangers without getting nervous or upset about it. Networking events don't have to be any different.

Break it into Pieces

Many people find themselves overwhelmed at a networking event when there is a large group of strangers. Here's a secret: you don't have to talk to everyone. In fact, it's impossible! Unless you are up on stage speaking to the masses, you simply cannot talk to everyone in the room in the short time you have. I have noticed at many dinner parties that if there are more than six people in an unstructured group (with no one leading a conversation for everyone to listen to), there will be more than one conversation going on at a time. Realize that at a networking mixer you are only going to be talking to a maximum amount of five people at a time. Most of the time, you will be talking to one to three people. Doesn't that seem like a more reasonable bite to chew?

Find an Ice Breaker

The scenario I used with my shy friend about finding Fred Flintstone is an Ice Breaker. It's something orchestrated by the person who planned the event/party to get people to walk around and talk to one another. Not every event has an Ice Breaker set up in advance, but you don't have to rely on the event planner. I suggest that you start with an Ice Breaker of your own. This is something that you can use to start a conversation with the people you meet. Try not to make the conversation too personal until you get to know someone better.

Some suggestions are things like:

- What do you do for a living?
- Why did you decide to come out to this networking event?
- Where did you grow up?
- What is your favorite TV show from your childhood?
- If you could have one superhuman ability, what would it be?
- Did you hear about <that thing on the news lately>?

Think about other Ice Breakers that you might be able to use and list them here.

Understanding your Audience

Most networking events have some reason for coming together. You should take care to understand who your audience is before you start to have a conversation with people.

Unless you are at an event where people there all have the same interests on a topic that you do, you should always introduce yourself at a simple level (something that a fifth grader would understand) and then see where the conversation goes from there.

Later on in this workbook, I will go over how to keep your conversation simple. For now, I challenge you to have simple introduction for yourself that you can then expand on later if you find that someone has interest in that topic.

Tips for the Shy Guy

I was originally going title this section something about introverts. The reality is that even extroverts, who get their energy from talking to people, can initially come off as shy in a conversation. Most people need a little boost to get going before they can break out of their shy shell.

Go with an Outgoing Friend

If you have trouble making new friends and introducing yourself to new people, find a friend who is outgoing to go to a networking event with you. People who are outgoing have no problem walking up to a crowd of strangers and starting a conversation. They will be happy to introduce you to anyone they meet.

My friend Mike, loves meeting new people. Most of the time we can't keep up with him, because he's off making a new friend. When he meets someone who he finds interesting, he brings that person back to his group of friends and introduces all of us to each other. I've met some of the most interesting people – many of whom I would never have otherwise met – because of the time that I have spent in social situations with Mike.

Look for Someone Who's Smiling

At my networking events, I always say that a smile starts a conversation. This is true whether you are at my networking event or not. All you really have to do is be approachable. If you see someone who's smiling and having a good time, you can always smile back at them and see if they respond. Sometimes people will act as though they did not notice you at all. More often than not at a networking event, they are just as interested in talking to new people as you are.

Find Events Focused on your Interest

It's much easier to network with strangers if the conversation is about something that you already have knowledge on. There are all kinds of networking events and meetup groups geared towards specific interests. If you don't know how to find these events find someone who has similar interests and ask them if they have a group of people that they meet with. If all else fails you can always create your own.

Arrive Early

If you are really shy at networking events, it's always a good idea to show up early. As the night goes on, people tend to migrate towards people they already know and it becomes more difficult to join a conversation. Many times at the beginning of an event you will encounter other people who are waiting for people they know to arrive. This gives you a great opportunity to introduce yourself and potentially get to meet their friends as they show up at the event.

Volunteer

Lots of networking events need volunteers in order to make the event run smoothly. Volunteering at an event makes you feel like you have a reason and a purpose to be there beyond just networking. I always ask people to work the front door for my events to greet people and welcome them as they come in. This gives people a chance to get to know someone as they are checking in for the event.

My friend Jim was a self-identified introvert. You wouldn't know it from meeting him now. When he first started coming to my events, he chose to work the door and greet people. Soon he started to feel like he was partially a host for the party. He always knew the answers to the questions that were necessary to make the event run (like "How do I use these drink tickets?" or "Where is the bathroom?"). He became known as the go-to guy. He then started to learn to introduce people to one another. One day he ran up to me, positively giddy. He had introduced two people who didn't know each other and they had a conversation for 30 minutes.

Working the Room

The next part of networking to consider is how to work the room.

Opening

I have a standard opening that I like to use when I have people make introductions. It's short, sweet and to the point.

At many networking events, you are asked to go around the room and make a 30 second introduction. So many times I see people blathering on about nothing in particular for 2 – 3 minutes. People start to get angry and frustrated because those individuals are stealing the time from everyone else in the room. They stop listening because they get upset. On the flipside, if someone can easily and effectively introduce themselves in less than 30 seconds people pay attention and listen. That individual may come off more confident than they probably feel.

At networking mixers, you meet lots of people and you introduce yourself multiple times. Your elevator pitch may be hard to work into your natural introduction, so you need an opening. (The elevator pitch comes in handy once you decide to continue the conversation.)

I suggest that for both your 30 second intro as well as you when you are introducing yourself to someone new to follow this format:

1) Your Name
2) Your Functional Area (sales, marketing, tech, etc)
3) Your Current Company (or you can state "I was formerly with _____")
4) An "I AM" Statement
5) How you Add Value by being that

Your Name is self-explanatory.

Your Functional Area is used to frame your perspective on things. You can also use your title if it makes sense. You may want to stay away from titles, however, because so many companies use titles that are confusing.

Your Current Company is used again to frame your perspective on things. If you work for a big well known company that means something to people. If you work for a smaller company you can always say something like "I work for a small company who builds mobile applications." If you are a job seeker, the phrase "I was formerly with _____" helps to frame your perspective and also lets people know you are looking for a new opportunity without sounding too desperate.

Your I AM statement is a statement that you can make in 3 – 5 words that helps to describe who you are enough to know whether or not to continue a conversation with you. Your I AM is not a title *per se*. I encourage you to get very descriptive about it. Sometimes I hear people say "I am a project manager" or "I am a people-person;" those phrases are so overused that they don't really paint a good picture of who you are and what you do. Consider things like "I AM a manager of monkeys" or "I AM a technology fire-starter" or "I AM a finance guru." The point is to clearly paint a memorable picture.

Your VALUE statement is one clear concise sentence on how you add value by being whatever it is that you said you are.

A statement that I will frequently use is:

Hello, I'm Kim Brushaber. I am the CEO of Bridge ATX, a local networking group. I am a connector. I connect individuals to Austin Businesses and Austin Businesses to the Austin Community.

I choose to use my title of CEO because there are too many functional areas that I cover to list them all out.

When I was a programmer I could have used:

Hello, I'm Kim Brushaber. I am working in technology for a local startup company. I am technology triage. I put the bandages on our software until the development team has time to go back and create a permanent solution.

Let's work on yours:

Your Name   Hello My Name Is
Your Title /
Functional Area
Your Company
I AM statement
Value statement

Get out and practice frequently. It has been rare for me to hear someone who can come up with their introduction so simply and perfectly on the first try. It takes time to figure out what rolls out of your mouth smoothly and clearly. Feel free to change it up if it isn't working for you or if you get bored with it.

Story Telling

Once you have delivered your introduction and you have covered your elevator speech, it's time to continue the conversation. Sometimes you will flow easily into conversation with someone based on some commonalities that you both have.

Sometimes you will determine from the introduction that you have nothing in common and it's time to move onto another conversation. If you want to continue the conversation, you should always be prepared with a few stories that you can tell in order to keep the conversation going. This is especially true if you are not a natural conversationalist or story teller.

For networking, I like to consider two different types of storytelling:

- Basic
- Memorable

It's good to have one of each prepared or at least outlined so you can carry the conversation.

If you are having difficulties telling your story there is an entire workbook dedicated to this conversation entitled "Identifying your Dream Job – And Telling your Story to Get It".

Basic

Basic stories are stories that are really just used to spark a conversation. These stories are something that anyone that you meet can follow and contribute to. Until you get to know someone better, you want to stay away from anything too personal or too controversial. You want this to be short and sweet and to the point.

I like to share the story of how I went from being a techie to a recruiter. Something like:

For twelve years, I worked in technology. I started my career as a Java Developer. I'm one of those people who get bored pretty easily if I am stuck doing the same thing. So I bounced around every couple of years in a variety of different roles within the software company where I worked. One day I read the book Eat, Pray, Love and it changed my life. I decided that I needed to be doing something that helped people more directly. A friend of mine ran a recruiting business and he thought I would be a natural tech recruiter because I had worked with staffing technology before. I also had the social skills to get out and talk to people and meet with them. I thought it would be a great opportunity for me to make a difference daily in people's lives. So, that's how I ended up working in recruiting.

From this story people might continue the conversation with:

- My Inner Computer Geek
- Getting Bored Easily
- Talking about the popular book – Eat, Pray, Love
- Making a Career Change
- Making a Difference in People's Lives
- The Current State of the Job Market

Think of some basic stories from your life that you might be willing to share with a total stranger in order to get a conversation started. Use the space below to jot down some references that you can use to create your stories.

Select your favorite basic story from above and see if you can write out the story (in regular handwriting) to fit in the box below.

Memorable

People will be able to bond with you more quickly if you can appeal to their empathy. Telling a story that evokes an emotion makes it more memorable and therefore you are more memorable. If someone connects and bonds with you, they will frequently have additional stories to share as well.

While a sad story can definitely be memorable, you don't want to make strangers sad at a networking event. Instead I recommend coming up with a story that's funny or uplifting. Again, take care not to share anything too personal or too uncomfortable.

For a while, I had two almost celebrities in an executive networking job clublet that I ran. I say almost celebrities because they both had a famous name. Each Tuesday morning I would listen to Michael Jordan (who is not the basketball player) and Ann Taylor (who is not the clothes designer) introduce themselves to the group by making fun of their famous names. Michael told me a funny story once about how he was running late at the airport to catch a connecting flight. When he got to the second flight's gate he discovered that they had held his flight for him and they had upgraded him to First Class because of his name. It didn't hurt that the connecting flight was in Chicago.

This was a great story for Michael to tell because people can understand why there might be confusion. It has a funny twist to it. But most of all, people are not going to forget his name. Or at least when he introduces himself again, people will remember that story.

Not all of us can be blessed with a celebrity name for our memorable stories. However, we all have stories that we can tell that can be amusing to other people. If you're not naturally one of "the funny guys," you can make your story memorable by talking about something that impressed you or made your proud.

Think of some memorable stories from your life that you might be willing to share with a total stranger in order to get a conversation started.

Use the space below to jot down some references that you can use to create your stories.

Select your favorite memorable story from above and see if you can write out the story (in regular handwriting) to fit in the box below.

Building Rapport

If you want to continue to build bridges and make the connections with the people that you meet at a networking event, it is important to establish rapport with them. This is the fancy way of saying they either need to like you, or at least respect you.

Here are some quick tips to help you to build better rapport:

Be Genuine

I'm not sure if this is as important in other cities as it is in Austin, Texas. In Austin, people are as genuine as they come. If you aren't genuine, people sense it immediately. Their little spidey senses go off and they know that you aren't being completely honest. It's almost impossible to build real rapport with people if you aren't being truthful. This doesn't mean you have to spill all your family's deepest darkest secrets. It simply means that whatever you choose to say or talk about should be told with as much of your true self as you can muster.

Listen

People feel better about people who listen to them. This doesn't mean you should simply hear what they are saying. Instead, you should listen *and* respond thoughtfully to the things that they tell you.

I was once being interviewed for a job. When I went into the interview, all the interviewer talked about was the company and the role and why it would be so wonderful for me to work there. I barely told him anything about me. I asked him thoughtful questions based on the information that he was giving me. At the end of the interview, I thought I had bombed it for sure because I never had an opportunity to tell him anything about what I could do for his company. He came back and told me that it was the best interview he had ever had.

Sometimes, people just need people to listen to them.

Do take caution though not to let them completely occupy the entire conversation. Remember that you are out networking for a reason as well and you want to make sure that you communicate with your goal in mind. If you can communicate it quickly and effectively (in your introduction) then you really don't need to say more and you can have the time to really listen.

Write Things Down

Unless you have a photographic memory, it is important to take time to write down your impressions of your conversations the first chance that you have. Some people are able to do this immediately with apps on their smart phones. Some people will jot down little memorable notes on the business cards they collect. If you can't do either of these things, take the first opportunity you can after the networking event to sit and recall your memories from the event. Being able to refer to these notes later can help you to remember who it was that you talked to. It also is a great conversation starter for the next time that you reach out to them.

Find Commonalities

It's always easier to remember someone if you find that you have something in common. It's also easier to continue a conversation with someone. Sometimes this can prove to be challenging. However, I have found that eventually you can find something in common with everyone (even if it is the fact that you both hate networking).

The People You Network With

Networking Amongst Friends and Family

Friends and family can be one of the most valuable tools in your networking toolkit. They already know you and care about you. They have a vested interest in seeing you reach your goals. They are going to understand details about you and your personality that casual acquaintances won't. If you ask them for a favor, they will help you.

Friends and family naturally want to help you. If you ask for something that is unclear and uncertain, they feel bad because they don't know how to help you. If you ask them for something that is clearly stated, they can easily assess whether or not they can help you.

For example

If you say, "I'm looking for a Tech Writer position," your friends and family may not understand what a Tech Writer does. They don't know who might want to hire a Tech Writer. They'll keep their ears open for you, but the chances of them being successful are not great. This will make them feel bad and it will hurt your cause. Eventually, they may even start to avoid you because they know they don't know how to help.

If you say, "I'm looking to talk to Silicon Labs about a Tech Writer position they posted," your friends and family can go through the mental rolodex and see if they know anyone at Silicon Labs. It's a much easier "yes" or "no" response. They can quickly determine whether or not they can help you. If they are out and about, they can listen for something very specific. If they run into a discussion about Silicon Labs, their minds will trigger and they will remember that you were talking about that company. They may even meet someone from there and return home with a business card from Silicon Labs.

My mom, bless her heart, will do anything she can to help me to succeed. If she doesn't have a clear picture of what I need help with, she'll start offering anything she can think of. If I'm not clear enough to her about what I really want, it's really no help at all, and I have to go back to her and say, "Thanks, but that's not really going to help me." In the past, she would set up appointments on my behalf. However, when I would talk to the other individual and I would discover within 5 minutes that we can't help each other and we're stuck in uncomfortable silence for the next 55 minutes. My mom wasn't doing anything wrong, she thought she was helping. It was me that was unclear in my request.

Your friends and family can be your best cheerleaders. They will go the extra mile to help you, no matter what it may take. Start to channel your energy in a very focused direction and you will start to see results.

I talk to job seekers on a frequent basis. Their friends and family know that they are looking for a job. They think that they are being helpful when they mention that they saw that Staples was hiring. As a job seeker you don't want just any job, you want a specific job. You need to be clear about telling your friends and family about what you want.

We all have friends who we interact with on a regular basis. Sometimes it's meeting with a friend over lunch. Sometimes it's sitting next to a friend at a ball game. Sometimes it's grabbing a drink.

When you have already established rapport with someone, be sure to quickly determine if your friend can help you get what you need.   That way you can easily and freely move onto whatever other topic of conversation flows freely while you are together. Be sure to write down how they can help you (if they can) and follow up!

Your conversation with your friend can be as short, simple and painless as that. Do not draw out the conversation any longer than it has to be to produce the results – a connection. If your friend has more questions for you, feel free to answer them but don't force information on them. Of course, follow up!

See if you can clearly state your networking goals in the box below. Have your friends and family repeat back to you what your goals are to make sure that they understand how they can help to connect you to the right opportunities. Don't rule out your family because you don't know who they might encounter.

Networking With Strangers

Networking with strangers can happen in a variety of different places. It may be a formal networking event. It may be an informal conversation. This is the time to pull out your elevator pitch.

After you have delivered your elevator pitch, pause. Wait to see if someone is interested in talking more about what you have just said. If their eyes glass over and they politely smile at you, back away. If they ask you questions and want more information from you, that's where you have the opportunity to provide it. Be conscious of time. Every 2 minutes, pause, and give them an opportunity to politely excuse themselves from the conversation if necessary.

There is a grace in politely dislodging yourself from a conversation. We have all been trapped in the never ending story. When you are networking with strangers, it is essential that you use your time to the best of your advantage. Pulling yourself away from a conversation is quite the art form in itself. It helps if you have a few escape phrases planned.

Common phrases might be:

- "I've really enjoyed this conversation, but I am here to network this evening. Do you think we could make time to talk more about this later?"
- "I've really enjoyed this conversation, but it's difficult to hear in this room. Could we set up some time for coffee to discuss this further?"
- "Thank you so much for your time. I've appreciated this conversation. Can I have your card?"
- "It was really great to meet you. I need to talk to <my friend who just game in the room>. Would you please excuse me?"
- "Thank you very much. Please excuse me while I go meet more people."
- "It seems my drink is now empty. Please excuse me while I go refill it. Enjoy your evening"

Once you have established enough rapport with a person to determine that you would like to have a future conversation with them – then and only then – should you give them one of your business cards. When you decide to continue a conversation with a stranger, be very sensitive to the amount of time they have available. If possible, find a way for you both to benefit from the conversation.

Networking With Experts

Experts on particular subjects have a variety of different people who always want to "pick their brain" in return for a cup of coffee. A lot of times these experts charge an hourly fee for their help and assistance. Do not be upset if they tell you that they don't have time to meet with you for a cup of coffee or the price of lunch. If you had to choose between people paying you $150 an hour for your time or meeting someone for a cup of coffee, what would you choose? Be respectful of taking time away from someone whose time is in high demand.

If you do get someone to agree to meet with you:

- Agree to meet on their schedule
- Come prepared with everything you need for the discussion
- Arrive early for the meeting
- Stay focused on the discussion at hand
- Send a gracious thank you note after the meeting (email or a physical note are find depending on your preference)
- Follow up promptly on anything they ask you to do

Networking with your Target Company

On some occasions you will actually run into someone who works for one of your target companies. Remember that you have done your research and you know about what is going on within this company. Be friendly and cordial. Get to the point quickly. Get the information that you need, set up an outside meeting (if possible) and then turn the conversation back onto them. People feel like they had a much better conversation if they have the opportunity to do most of the talking. Let them decide if they want to go into details on the help you're seeking at that moment or if you should set up another time to talk.

Closing

Closing out your conversation is just as important as your introduction. This is the way that people are going to remember you.

If you find that you are having a great conversation with someone who you are networking with, be sure to set up a time outside of the networking event to talk further. Networking events are really bad for having deeper conversations because they are frequently noisy and distracting. You also want to be sure to make time at the networking events in order to meet your goals. The people you are networking with have goals and agendas as well, so you don't want to occupy too much of their time.

Sometimes when you are talking to someone another person will join the conversation as well. When you feel that you are done with the conversation it is time to excuse yourself from the conversation so that you can continue to network with other people.

If you feel that a good connection was made, be sure to exchange contact information and set a time for follow up in the future.

Politely Escaping a Conversation

Frequently, you will find yourself in a conversation where the conversation is no longer meeting your goal OR the goal has already been met. In order to continue to meet your networking goal of the evening, you must learn how to gracefully free yourself from a conversation.

Sometimes this can be as easy as thanking someone for their help and exchanging business cards for follow up. A natural networker will have already dismissed themselves from the conversation before you've even had the chance to realize it.

Sometimes, however, your conversation partner may not pick up on cues to end the conversation. How can you remove yourself from a conversation where the other person does not want to end it yet? You need to make sure that you don't spoil any rapport that you have already built with the individual. The best way to do this is to practice a few scenarios. Know what you are going to do in advance should the situation come up.

Whatever your polite escape strategy, always leave the conversation on a good note. Make sure that any follow up items are clear between the two of you. Then move to your next conversation.

In one of my networking classes, I had a rather attractive young salesman named Shean tell us one of his stories when we approached this topic. Shean said he was at a networking event and that someone was occupying all of his attention for far too long. He had a drink and decided to finish it quickly in order to have an excuse to walk away from the conversation. The other person didn't get the hint. So Shean tried to excuse himself to go purchase another drink. The other person decided it was time for him to get another drink as well so he followed Shean to the bar. When Shean got to the bar he decided all of a sudden that he needed to hit the men's room. The other guy thought that was a good idea as well so took the conversation onto the men's room. You can only imagine how uncomfortable things became at this point. Upon leaving the men's room, Shean had had enough. He finally had to break down and tell this guy that he was becoming very uncomfortable with the situation.

Although, I'm sure that the stories are out there, I haven't heard of a tougher situation to break free from a conversation at a networking event. Typically the sign of exchanging business cards or a hand on someone to pause them is enough of a hint to wrap up the conversation.

When I'm running my networking classes, I normally have someone volunteer to break free of a conversation with me. I've become very good at being that annoying person you can't break free from. I will talk nonstop about nonsensical things without pausing for a breath or for them to interject. Frequently, my student will move to get away from me and I'll follow them through the room, jabbering on like a monkey. I've seen students use all kinds of tactics to break free before I finally have mercy on them and tell them they have had enough. I can't be that annoying in a workbook format, but I think it's instructive to understand why I do it.

Some of the tactics that I have seen people use to break free in that exercise are:

- Placing their hand on my arm or hand as if to physically try to stop me
- Handing me their business card and attempting to leave the conversation
- Attempting to interrupt me (I make this difficult to do)
- Introducing me to a friend in the room
- Leaving the room
- Making up a fake phone call
- Placing obstacles like furniture in between us

Although, most of the time people try to politely struggle through the exercise hoping for me to take a breath long enough for them to escape the conversation.

I go through this exercise in workshops because students learn some effective tactics in getting rid of pests. I also do it because I know that they are never going to come across anyone as hard to get rid of as I am for that few minutes where I hound them for a conversation. After me, getting out of any other conversation seems so much easier.

Simple tactics such as excusing yourself from the conversation, extending a business card or simply bringing them to meet the next person you intend to talk to will end a conversation with most people.

Follow Up

It is very important to follow up with people within a week of meeting them at a networking event. Any longer than that and you risk the chance of them forgetting who you are. If you have a talking point to include that will allow them to remember the conversation, you have a better chance of them remembering that they said they would help you.

I used to go to the Super Computing Conferences. These conferences were filled with men and women in blue shirts and khaki pants (typical attire for business casual and trade shows). I would walk around the floor in a hot pink sweater in order to make myself stand out in the sea of blue. When I was following up with everyone, I would point out that I was the woman who was walking around in a pink sweater. (I'm not sure if I can do that anymore since I let you in on my little secret.) I do not advise men to walk around these events in a hot pink sweater. You do still want to appear professional. I do suggest that you do something that is professional that lets you stand out from the crowd. I had one group of aspiring networkers find a big blue fist that was a promotional item that doubled as a koozie, to their events during SXSW. It was the talk of the night. Just make sure that whatever you pick fits with your personality.

For job seekers, if the contact has asked you to send them a resume and there is a specific job at their company, this is your opportunity for you to go back to the job description and list out bullet point by bullet point why you are a perfect fit. It is a great way to showcase yourself while you are still fresh on their mind.

Each Moment Counts

Time kills all deals. I've seen some people send out follow up messages directly from an event. A well written message will work for that. Although, you do have to take care not to come off too desperate. Instead, I suggest that you follow up within a day or two after the event.

If you don't have something specific to say or you are still gathering information, you can send a simple "it was nice to meet you" email. If you intend to follow up again within a timeframe then you can take the opportunity to outline that timeframe at that point.

Asking for Referrals

Once you have established a good level of rapport with someone, it's a perfect time to ask for referrals. Hopefully you have done a good job communicating why you were networking in the first place. In your follow up you should ask the individual if they know of any additional people for you to talk to. Ideally, you would like two to three referrals per person. If you haven't established enough rapport yet, you may not get any. People are protective of their contacts (as they should be). Once you have established a good level of rapport in the future, you can ask for the referrals again.

When you get a referral, be sure to ask them why they referred that person to you. This helps you when you are trying to make that connection to the other person.

Making it Personal

Of course, you don't want to include any information that you haven't already discussed with the individual. If you went out and cyber stalked them after you met them, you probably don't want to let them know that unless you told them you would in advance.

I have a friend who is known for doing thorough research before meeting with an individual. She works in a marketing capacity so she has been trained to be very detail oriented and she is really good at her job. She would scour the web looking for information on the individual that she was meeting with in order to have some conversation points during her meeting. I received feedback after one of her meetings that the gentleman that she had met with felt like he had been stalked. My friend had discussed things he didn't even know were out on the web. It left him feeling violated that she knew so much of his private information before he had even met her for the first time.

You should have enough information from the conversation to make them feel as though they are remembered.

Once I met someone at one of my networking events. I discussed with him my perspective on how to network effectively. The next day I received an email from him that was obviously a form letter that said he was happy to meet me recently (didn't even mention my event) and that he wanted me to know about his services. Since he knew that I help people to network, I felt inclined to send him a response. I picked apart his email and told him how impersonal I found it. I also found it tacky that he was promoting his services to me before I even suggested that I wanted them. I ran into him again at another networking event. He laughed it off and told me that he expected a response like that from me. We both let things go back to neutral, but he was never able to reestablish rapport with me again. I talked to other people who had received the same email; they ignored his email without commenting about it. All his hard work of meeting people at a networking event was washed down the drain because he chose to send a canned response with nothing personal in it at all. Had he written the tiniest personalization into the note before he went into his spiel, it would have at least have been salvageable. Instead his actions made me feel like I was just another business card captured in his pile.

People want to feel like they are special and they are remembered if they have talked to you for more than ten minutes.

I had another case where I met someone at a networking event. He was looking for a new job and completely dominated our conversation, doing nothing but talk about himself. The next time I met him, he completely forgot that he had met me before. I met him a third time, and again he didn't remember me. So, I chose not to follow up with him. A few months later, I received an email via LinkedIn that he wanted to connect with me with no suggestion of a personal connection to me. The fourth time I met him in person, he tried to introduce himself again and my professionalism slipped. I coldly looked at him and told him I knew exactly who he was. I went on to outline the previous times that we met and the LinkedIn email that I received. To his credit, after the fourth meeting he took the time to write me a rather lengthy explanation for his actions. He never forgot me again. Unfortunately, he had already lost my trust.

Do not interpret this to mean that I am all high and mighty and believe that everyone must remember me. I meet hundreds of people a month and will admit that I don't remember them all. I don't follow up with people unless there is a clear action to take on my part or theirs. I simply point out the two examples above because they represent extreme cases and I don't want any of you to fall into these pitfalls.

On the flipside, when people do remember me and they remember what I talked to them about I am always flattered. When people take the time to include a small little note about how we met or what we talked about, I am very appreciative.

People have difficulties remembering names. Sometimes they even have difficulty remembering faces. However, most people will remember stories, especially if you show them that you took the time to remember theirs.

Make it Easy to Help You

The two things that you need to have to make networking a success are:

- Familiarity
- Ease of Assistance

Familiarity

When you are at a networking event, you really can't control familiarity that well. You either know the person already or you don't. However, the more familiar someone is with you, the more likely they will remember to help you. If you frequently attend the same events you may run into the same people that you've met before.

Think about this one – "How many times would you have to meet someone before you'd be willing to pick them up from the airport in the middle of the night?" Would that be 5 times, 10 times, one long lunch conversation? The more rapport you build, the more likely they are going to help you in whatever way you need help.

Ease of Assistance

The easier it is to help you, the more likely it will be for someone to do it. Think of ways to ask your contacts for help. Don't make them work for it.

A common way to ask people for help is to request an email introduction. In this case, you simply ask your contact to put you in touch with one of their contacts over email. If they know you well enough and can trust that you will be nice to their contact, then they will be happy to do so. You should also include a few statements about why you want to talk to the other person.

When you're at a networking event, you can ask your contact to help you get introduced to various different people. They may know who to put you in touch with and introduce you directly to that person at the event.

Look for Opportunities to Help Them

Another way to feel more comfortable when out networking is to find ways to help the other individual. It's much easier to ask someone for help if you know that you will be returning the favor. If you are meeting someone for the first time, try and make sure that the conversation is equally about them as it is about you. In fact, if you have already met your event networking goal in talking to them, you can let the conversation be more about the other individual or about something that you mutually find interesting. Through the conversation, you may find that you have met someone else at that same event that you can introduce them to.

People Want to Be the Hero

I've talked to many people who are afraid to ask for help if they believe they have nothing to give in return. The reality is that sometime in the future they will likely be able to help very effectively. Unfortunately, this does little to calm their fears in the moment.

Imagine that you are the one who is in the position to help. Let's say that Jack wants to meet Sue and you are the connection standing between them. Jack comes to you and says that he really wants to meet Sue because he thinks he can help Sue. He goes on to explain briefly and clearly exactly what his intentions are. You can see in Jack's explanation that Sue does in fact need Jack based on his explanation and what you know about Sue. You then introduce Sue to Jack by forwarding his summary of how he can help Sue. Sue takes a look at this and admits that she is in fact looking for help from someone like Jack. Now all of a sudden you are the hero to Sue because you helped her find a solution to her problem. You are also the hero to Jack because you made the introduction to Sue. Every time you run into Sue or Jack they rave about how great it was for you to put Sue and Jack in touch with one another. How good does that make you feel?

My story of you, Sue and Jack is repeated on a daily basis where I stand in your place. If I feel that Jack has clearly communicated how he can help Sue and I know that Sue needs Jack's help, I will always make that introduction.

So, you see, even though you may be in Jack's shoes, you have made that middle man the hero. Doesn't everyone want to be a hero?

Marking your Calendar for Reminders

Sometimes your initial follow up isn't enough to get a response. This is especially the case if you follow up after a major event where the person you are contacting has met several people in a short period of time. Most of the time, they will see your response but their ability to respond back to it is diminished by whatever fire is raging in front of them at the moment. Depending on the day, I may have a dozen fires distracting my attention.

I always encourage people that if they need something from someone else, follow up with them a second time. If I am the one who needs a connection or an action to be taken, I will place a reminder on my calendar for a week from the initial contact. It will say something like "Follow up with Tom" and in the body of the calendar I'll include my previous email to them so that I don't have to go and look it up later. This can be done with phone calls as well; you'll just have to summarize the conversation. When the action is completed, I'll remove the reminder from my calendar. If a week passes and I have not received a response, I will go back and send a follow up email and include my original email.

Frequency – Treat it Like Dating

People often ask me how often they should continue to follow up.   I simply say to treat it like dating. This means you don't want to come across too desperate but you do want them to know that you are interested.

If you just wanted to say, "It was nice to meet you," no follow up is necessary until you meet each other again.

If you have an action for them to take that is not immediate then you can reach out to them once to remind them and a second time to remind them again a week later.

If you have an action that does need immediate attention, you can reach out a little more frequently.

The frequency all depends on how well you know them and how you perceive that they feel about you.

Allow Them to "Bail Out"

If you find that after a couple repeated attempts you don't receive a response from the other person, you should offer them the opportunity to "bail out" on your request. People can talk big at networking events promising that they can do something. They aren't normally lying about it, but in the light of day when the moment is over they realize that they promised something they are not comfortable with. They may realize that they promised you that they would introduce you to their boss and then their boss comes in and says they are tired of all these random introductions. There's any number of reasons why a person may decide later that they can't commit to their promises. If you don't care if you burn that bridge then you can press them harder. I suggest that you always strive to preserve the bridge. Give the other individual an opportunity to opt out of their promise and salvage the relationship for a future day and time.

Remain Visible

If you're job hunting or responsible for sales for a company, you want to make sure that you remain visible. Out of sight, out of mind can frequently occur with networking. Remaining visible is especially important if you are in job search mode or if you are starting a new business. People think because they haven't heard from you that you don't need them anymore. In both of those cases it's important to keep up with your best contacts on a more regular basis.

I try to pay attention to things that may be of interest to my contacts. If I remember their birthday, I'll send them a birthday note. If I see that their company is doing something interesting, I'll send them congratulations. I want to be sure that they know I am thinking of them without being overly pushy.

On a quarterly basis, I like to update my whole contact list with the activities that I am taking. I don't like to send form style letters very often, but I want to make sure to keep everyone up to date. I use a newsletter format that allows people to opt out if they aren't interested. Then I try to send a simple email that states what I've been up to and how I might be able to help people.

Even before I ran my own business, I used to look over my Outlook contacts and see who I hadn't talked to in a while. I would send them an email just to let them know I was thinking about them. I suppose I have become a bit lazy about that with Facebook. I just assume that everyone keeps up with me on that now. If I'm curious what people are up to, I can always look up their Facebook account if they are friends with me. Others I'll still send a short note every once in a while.

Pick Two Events to go to Each Month

I always tell people to find two networking events that they will commit to going to every month. You can certainly go to more, but those two events will help you to keep your networking skills up to date. It will also help you to establish rapport amongst those friends.

This can become more challenging if your life becomes busy and complicated. However, it is much harder to start the momentum again if you stop for any period of time.

Finding Networking Events

Meetup groups, like www.meetup.com, are spread all over the nation. They are a great place to find people interested in doing something that interests you.

Many cities have online calendars that refer to events that you are able to attend. Additionally, there are individuals who keep up lists of their favorite networking events and publish them online or in newsletters.

Most recurring networking events will have a mailing list or distribution to let people know that the event is happening again.

If all else fails, ask people who you consider to be heavy duty networkers how they find out about the events that they attend.

Generational Differences

Different generations communicate in different ways. Baby Boomers typically cannot let a phone ring without answering it. Generation X has spent most of their adult life on email. Generation Y and Millennials like the more abbreviated instant information of text messages.

Following up with individuals can be a challenge because of different people's favorite forms of communication. It's always a good idea to ask someone how they prefer to interact. Sometimes you'll have someone leave a message on their cell phone to say that if you want to reach them you should email them or text them.

Just because you like to communicate in one form or fashion, do not assume that with the person you are interacting with prefers the same form. Be flexible, and you will build rapport.

Social Media and Blogging

What Is Social Media?

Even the concept of what social media is changing every day. Social media is a way to use online communications to interact with others in a mass format. We've gone from simply putting information out there to interacting with that information.

There are a variety of tools available that are part of social media.

Some social media tools are:

- Facebook
- LinkedIn
- Twitter
- Flickr (photos)
- YouTube
- SlideShare
- Blogs
- Delicious (bookmarks)
- Digg (links)
- MailChimp, iContact, ConstantContact, Emma (software used for automating newsletters)

There are many others, but you get the point. ☺

Why You Should Use Social Media?

In my opinion, social media can be used successfully in one of two manners:

- To Communicate to the Masses
- To Become Known as the Expert

Communicating to the Masses

Never before has it been so easy to reach out to all of your friends and family and contacts with the simple touch of a button.

When I went to my 10 year high school reunion, I felt so uncomfortable and so out of place. I looked at these people were such an important part of my life for four years. I knew their names and their faces, but I couldn't remember a single thing about them. It was as if I had an uncomfortable form of amnesia. Everyone else at the reunion felt the same, unless they had a small group of people that they had remained in touch with over the last 10 years. We all quickly raced to the bar to numb the discomfort and awkwardness that we were feeling.

I already know that the 20 year high school reunion will be completely different, because of Facebook, I now know so many of their personal stories. I know where they have been on vacation. I know their children's names. I know their thoughts and their personalities. I know their story. I get tiny little quips now and again from them. If they say something that I can relate to, I can quickly respond back with my own thoughts on the subject. When I go back to my 20 year high school reunion, I will go back to a group of friends who I have kept up with online. And they've kept up with me.

The ability to know everyone's personal story is the key to helping people who you've lost touch with (or sometimes never met) find whatever it is that they are looking for.

Becoming an Expert (Branding)

Social media allows you to become known as an expert without even leaving the comfort of your home. As you begin to contribute your thoughts and ideas out to the internet, you will start to get a following of people who come to know you as an expert in your field. This can catapult you into a new job or possibly a temporary contract position.

Blogs

You can get a free Wordpress (www.wordpress.org) application to talk about anything you want. A Blog for example. You can use Twitter (www.twitter.com) to rebroadcast your blogs. You can use Tags in your blogs to become highly ranked in Google searches.

Getting the right person to notice you may catapult you into your next job. If you have a blog, include it on your business card.

The other advantage of blogs is that you can point prospective employers to your blog. They can then read the information that you have been putting out to the world and quickly grasp the fact that you are an expert on whatever topic you'd like.

Newsletters

Newsletters are similar to blogs, but a Newsletter is specifically pointed at an opt-in email address. You can use this forum to talk about your areas of expertise. For a little extra money, you can subscribe to a Newsletter tool that will manage the list for you and remove the bounces and allow people to subscribe or unsubscribe to your newsletter.

Connecting on LinkedIn

Many people stay in touch with their networking contacts via LinkedIn (www.LinkedIn.com). However, different people have different rules for who they are willing to connect to. Some people will automatically connect to anyone that asks to connect to them. Others will not connect to anyone unless they make the choice to do so.

If you find that you would like to connect with someone on LinkedIn, you should ask them first if it's okay to do so. One approach is to close out a networking conversation where you've established good rapport, with an invite to connect on LinkedIn. You'll get a warmer and fuzzier response that way. Sometimes I will send a link in my follow up emails that they can choose to connect with me if they would like to. That way it's up to them to put out the connection request.

LinkedIn can become a valuable resource in helping you to identify which of your contacts are connected to the people you want to network with.

Determining Who You Want To Talk To

When you are first starting to network, it's a good idea to identify who it is that you want to talk to.

Highly Connected Individuals

There are people in everyone's network who are connected to just about everyone. These are great people to leverage when you are looking to make connections. However, you must consider that many people are reaching out to those individuals to make introductions.

I am much more responsive to people who I've spent time with and have gotten to know. The tough part is finding the time to get to know me.

Highly networked individuals may take a little time for you to get to know them. However, once they like you and trust you, they will normally help you to get in touch with the people who you need to know.

People with Common Interests

People with common interests are always great to network with. You already have something in common with them. You will typically find that you have other things in common and friendships can be made quickly and easily.

Identifying Target Companies or Individuals

There are a lot of resources to help you come up with lists of companies to target. The Business Journals (www.bizjournals.com) have weekly lists that they distribute. Hoover's (www.hoovers.com) has a list that they publish. LinkedIn is great for both targeting companies and individuals.

The best resource is still word of mouth. Tell people about the kinds of companies you are interested in learning more about and most of them will have a few suggestions for you.

Working on your Messages and Stories

Keep It Simple

You may be the best Semiconductor Fabrication Wafer Designer in the universe. However, unless your friends and family work in the Semiconductor Industry, they will have no idea what you do. Chances are they will key off some words and get all wrong.

"My brother John, he works in Semiconductors. He has something to do with Fabric Softener. I'm not really sure."

When I worked as a Java Developer, I had people approach me all the time asking me what I did. My first response was always, "I work with computers." If I got a little nod and a smile, I realized that I had answered their question. However, a lot of time I would get, "I work with computers too. What do you do?" Then I knew I could take the conversation deeper.

When you are explaining what you do to your family and friends, keep it as simple as possible. Use terms that the average person can understand. It's okay if they don't know every last detail of what you do, they just have to know enough to help you get a conversation started.

I feel like you need some closure here. I did not realize this was the end of your book chapters!

NETWORK LIKE A PRO

APPENDIX

Example Letters and Conversations

Frequently at networking events you meet someone who agrees to make an introduction on your behalf. Below is an example of an email that you can modify to request that introduction. If you remember personal information from your conversation, it is always good to include it so that they have a frame of reference for your follow up.

Hello Jim –

It was so nice to meet you last night at the Social Media Club Event. I really enjoyed talking to you about your recent trip to Greece. I can't wait until I get a chance to go and explore it for myself.

Last night we talked about your friend David over at Oracle. You thought that he might be able to tell me some more about the Tech Writer position that they have posted. Thank you so much for agreeing to make that introduction. It will really help me in my job search.

Of course, if you run across any other Tech Writer positions out there, I would love to hear about them.

I look forward to bumping into you again soon!

Have a great week.

Kim

Then after this is sent, put a note on your calendar that says "Follow up with Jim on XX-XX-XX." Include his email address and the original email in case you need to reference it. If Jim hasn't followed up by then, send another email like:

Hey Jim –

I wanted to follow up with you. I sent you an email last Tuesday after the Social Media Club event that we attended together.

You had said you would put me in touch with your friend David over at Oracle. I know that people get busy and things slip their mind. I just wanted to send you a quick reminder.

If you have already spoken to David and he doesn't believe that this is a good connection for me, please let me know, so I can try to find another way to continue my search.

Again, thank you so much for agreeing to help me.

Let me know how I can return the favor for you.

Sincerely,

Kim

Notice how I left the opportunity to back out of the conversation. This is entirely intentional. Sometimes people make promises after a few drinks that they can't really deliver on. You'd rather give them the opportunity to back out if necessary than continue to make them feel uncomfortable.

If Jim does forward on your introduction request, make sure that you send Jim a nice response back to thank him for helping you. A handwritten note is even nicer than an email. However, at least you need to respond back with an email.

Sometimes, you simply want to establish/continue rapport for later. This is helpful because if you do contact them later, they can go back and search their email to find out when they talked to you before. You can also reference that email for yourself to remember how you met them. In which case the email might look something like:

Hello Jim –

It was so nice to meet you last night at the Social Media Club Event. I enjoyed talking to you about the Austin economic situation. I hope that we can run across each other again soon.

Please let me know if I can ever help you!

Thanks!

Kim

If you find that you are in a state of career transition or you are an entrepreneur who has a lot of changes to communicate it's always good to reach out to your friends and family every quarter (or every month) to let them know what you are doing and where you might be able to use your help.

Dear Friends and Family –

Thank you so much for all your support while I am in this state of Career Transition.

I'm feeling good about the process that I have been pursuing. Recently, I took a networking class that I think will help my Job Search tremendously. I now have some new ideas to think about and new ways to start contacting companies.

Thank you so much to Rich and Anna. Your help has kicked off an interview process that looks to be very promising. I hope to give you exciting news on that soon.

In the meantime, in case that opportunity does not pan out, I would like your assistance in helping me to find contacts at these organizations:

Company 1
Company 2
Company 3
Company 4
Company 5

Or any other organization that is addressing how companies should be interacting with all the new social media tools.

Any contacts that you might have would be greatly appreciated.

I hope to share some very good news with you soon!

Sincerely,

Kim

P.S. If you would like to stop receiving these emails, please let me know and I'll remove you from the list.

Remember to keep it up beat. Accent any wins you may have had. Acknowledge anyone who may have helped you (more people will help you if you identify them in your newsletter). Be clear in your request for help.